STRIDERS

T0326103

Bok's Splendid Display

SCHOLASTIC

Published in the UK by
Scholastic Education, 2024
Scholastic Distribution Centre, Bosworth Avenue,
Tournament Fields, Warwick, CV34 6UQ
Scholastic Ireland, 89E Lagan Road, Dublin
Industrial Estate, Glasnevin, Dublin, D11 HP5F

1 2 3 4 5 6 7 8 9   4 5 6 7 8 9 0 1 2 3

Printed by Ashford Colour Press

The book is made of materials from well-managed,
FSC®-certified forests and other controlled sources.

MIX
Paper from
responsible sources
FSC FSC® C011748
www.fsc.org

A CIP catalogue record for this book is available
from the British Library.

ISBN 978-0702-32726-1

Author
Giles Clare

Editorial team
Rachel Morgan, Vicki Yates, Sasha Morton,
Jennie Clifford

Design team
Dipa Mistry, Andrea Lewis and We Are Grace

Photograph
p4 (background) vectopicta/Shutterstock

Illustrations
Berat Pekmezci/The Bright Agency

How to use this book

This book practises these letters and letter sounds:

ay (as in 'day')	ou (as in 'shouted')	ea (as in 'seat')
ir (as in 'bird')	ie (as in 'cried')	ue (as in 'blue')

Here are some of the words in the book that use the sounds above:

out   beat   twirling   display   true

This book uses these common tricky words:

was the of do to they all I my what have she he like come said he's putting you be me we love

About the series

This is the third book in a fiction series. In the first, Nick discovers Bok (an unusual bug) outside his house and decides to keep him as a pet. However, Bok causes problems when he keeps escaping.

Before reading

- Read the title and look at the cover. Discuss what the book might be about.
- Talk about the characters on page 4 and read their names.
- The story is split into chapters shown by numbers at the top of the page.

During reading

- If necessary, sound out and then blend the sounds to read the word: a-r-ou-n-d, around.
- Pause every so often to talk about the story.

After reading

- Talk about what has been read.

Mum

Nick

Nan

Bok

It was the first morning of the holidays.

The lid of Bok's plastic box was not sealed.
Bok had got out.

"That's annoying," cried Mum in dismay.
"Do not say a thing to Nan!"

They looked all around but Bok had vanished.

"This is his third attempt at getting away from us," sighed Nick.

The next day, a loud sound started to annoy Nan.

"I cannot hear my music," complained Nan.
Nick tried to see what it was.

"I have found Bok," shouted Nick.

Bok burst out from underneath Nan's seat.

Nan leaped out of her chair.
"My skirt!" she cried.

Bok beat his bright blue wings.
He fluttered like a bird around the room
and landed out of reach.

"Good boy, come down," pleaded Mum.

"Wait, he likes Nan's music," said Nick.
"He's twirling to the beat!"

swirl

sway

crouch

"He's putting on a display," said Mum.

"What do you think it means?" said Nick.

3

Mum was bothered about Bok.

"Keeping Bok as a pet may be cruel," she said.

"It's cruel to me," muttered Nan.
"But we love him!" cried Nick.

"Yes, but his disappearing, buzzing and display might be clues. He may wish he was out and free," said Mum.

Nick was about to argue, but he suspected this was true.